To dear Roy,

with love from Allison
xxx

Other books in this series:
Best Friends
Thank you Mum
I've got a crush on you
My Dad, My Hero
Stay Calm

Published in 2010 by Helen Exley Giftbooks in Great Britain. A copy of the CIP data is available from the British Library on request. All rights reserved. No part of this publication may be reproduced or transmitted in any form or by any means, electronic or mechanical, including photocopy, recording or any information storage and retrieval system without permission in writing from the Publisher.
Printed in China.

Words and illustrations © Jenny Kempe 2010
Design and arrangement © Exley Publications 2010
The moral right of the author has been asserted.

12 11 10 9 8 7 6 5 4 3 2 1

ISBN: 978-1-84634-495-4

Dedication: To the Wednesday Writers' Group.

Published by HELEN EXLEY®
Helen Exley Giftbooks, 16 Chalk Hill, Watford, Herts WD19 4BG, UK.
www.helenexleygiftbooks.com

Have a Perfect Day!

WORDS AND ILLUSTRATIONS BY

JENNY KEMPE

May today be full

of promise and possibility.

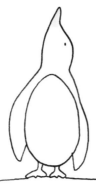

Today! I hope
someone gives you
a **BIG** thank you
– one you know you deserve.

May today be the day

you lose reserve and inhibition.

May today be the day you
will be recognised for
your achievements, big or small.

Let today be the day
you are surrounded by love.

Let today be the day
when nothing but sunshine
can get to you.

You know that thing
you always wanted to do,
but feared too much?

May today be
the day you do it.

Let today be the day you see
the bigger picture.

Let today be the day you
let go of an old grudge
and find trust in a friend.

Let today be the day you
feel deeply happy
– just to be alive.

In your busy life, I hope
that you can find
some time to just be.

May today take you away

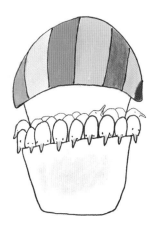

on a stomach-tickling adventure.

Let today be the day
you discover
the wonders of the world
right on your doorstep.

Do you have a couple of
seriously good friends?
Let today be
the day you tell them.

Today I hope somebody will be
very kind to you.

Let today be the day
you accept everything you are,
and everything you are not.
Let today be the day you discover
you are unique and perfect,
just the way you are.

Have a Perfect

Day.

Jenny Kempe

In 2009, overwhelmed by the endless bad news in the
media, Jenny Kempe decided to take a six month break
from newspapers, TV and radio. She turned her focus to
the things in life that made her happy; to friends and family
and to "taking time to just be". The result is the wonderfully
bright and positive gift book series "Life is Beautiful". Each
title has been designed to warm your heart and to put
a smile on your face. As gifts, these books will brighten up
the day, or even the life, of someone you care for.

About Helen Exley gifts

Helen Exley products cover the most powerful range of all human relationships: love between couples, the bonds within families and between friends. No expense is spared in making sure that each book is as thoughtful and meaningful a gift as it is possible to create: good to give, good to receive. You have the result in your hands. If you have loved it – tell others!

Visit our website to see all of Helen Exley's other books and gifts: **www.helenexleygiftbooks.com**

Helen Exley Giftbooks
16 Chalk Hill, Watford, Herts
WD19 4BG, UK
www.helenexleygiftbooks.com

We loved making this book for you.
We hope you'll enjoy the other titles
in our series Life is Beautiful.

The Life is Beautiful Team